Colores de la vida

Mexican Folk Art Colors in English and Spanish

Cynthia Weill

Folk Art by **Artisans** from **Oaxaca**

SCHOLASTIC INC.

RED

***

Rojo

Yellow

* * * * *

Amarillo

BLUE

✿ ✿ ✿ ✿ ✿ ✿

AZUL

GREEN

VERDE

Orange

※ ※ ※ ※ ※

Anaranjado

PINK

ROSADO

URPLE

✷ ✷ ✷ ✷ ✷

ORADO

TURQUOISE

TURQUESA

BROWN

❖ ❖ ❖ ❖ ❖

CAFÉ

BLACK

✿ ✿ ✿ ✿ ✿

NEGRO

WHITE

* * * * * *

BLANCO

GRAY

* * * * * *

GRIS

GOLD

* * * * *

DORADO

Silver

✾ ✾ ✾ ✾ ✾

Plateado

Can you say all the colors in Spanish?

* * * * * *

¿Puedes nombrar todos los colores en inglés?

In the country of Mexico, there is a beautiful state called Oaxaca (wah-HA-kah). Oaxaca's folk artists make many crafts including wood carving, tin work, ceramics, and papier-mâché. Each piece in *Colores de la vida* was lovingly made by hand so that children can learn their colors in English and Spanish.

Home of woodcarver Julio Jiménez, La Unión

Dedication

To: Bruce, Vicky, Bryant, Alexander, Nicholas, and Mom: You are the colors of my life!

Photographs by

Otto Piron

Thanks to

Jaime Ruiz, Friends of Oaxacan Folk Art, José Miguel Moracho, Kirsten Darling, Janet Glass, Ruth Borgman, Myriam Chapman, Jan Asikainen, Jorge Luis Santiago, Casa Colonial in Oaxaca, Mexico.

The artisans represented in *Colores de la vida* are:

From San Martín Tilcajete
Piggies: Maria Jiménez
Cat: Jesús Sosa/Juana Vicente
Lion: Rubí Fuentes/Efraín Broa

From Oaxaca City
Fish, Chickens: Miguel Ángel Agüero
Dragon babies: Pedro Mendoza

From La Unión
Goats, Rabbits, Cows: Eloy Santiago
From San Bártolo Coyotepec
Spider: Carlomagno Pedro Martínez
From Ocotlán
Sun: Apolinar Aguilar

From Arrazola
Possums: Moisés Jiménez
Lizard: Mario Castellanos
Polar Bears: Eleazar Morales
Giraffes: René Mandarín
From Atzompa
Musicians: Angélica Vásquez

Cover and Book Design by

Sergio A. Gómez

ISBN 978-0-545-46135-1
Copyright © 2011 by Cynthia Weill.
All rights reserved. Published by Scholastic Inc., 557 Broadway, New York, NY 10012, by arrangement with Cinco Puntos Press.
SCHOLASTIC, SCHOLASTIC EN ESPAÑOL, and associated logos are trademarks and/or registered trademarks of Scholastic Inc.
12 11 10 9 8 7 6   16 17/0
Printed in the U.S.A.   40
First Scholastic printing, September 2012

Editor's note:
We have used "café" instead of "marrón" for the color "brown" because that is the preferred term in Oaxaca.

Nota del editor:
Hemos utilizado "café" en lugar de "marrón" para el color que en inglés es "brown" porque así se le dice comúnmente en Oaxaca.